Seeds

Elizabeth Austen

Seeds come in many sizes.

Seeds come in many shapes.

Seeds come in many colors.

Seeds need water to grow.

Seeds grow into new **plants**.

Then, the plants grow new seeds.

Wind can spread the seeds.

Animals can spread the seeds, too.

Seeds grow almost anywhere!

Let's Do Science!

What do seeds do? Try this!

What to Get

- ❑ 2 sandwich bags
- ❑ masking tape
- ❑ paper towels
- ❑ seeds

What to Do

1. Put a wet paper towel in one bag. Put a dry towel in the other bag.

2. Put a bean seed in each bag.

3. Tape both bags to a sunny window. Add water to the wet bag each day. Do not water the dry bag.

4. After two weeks, check the seeds. What happened?

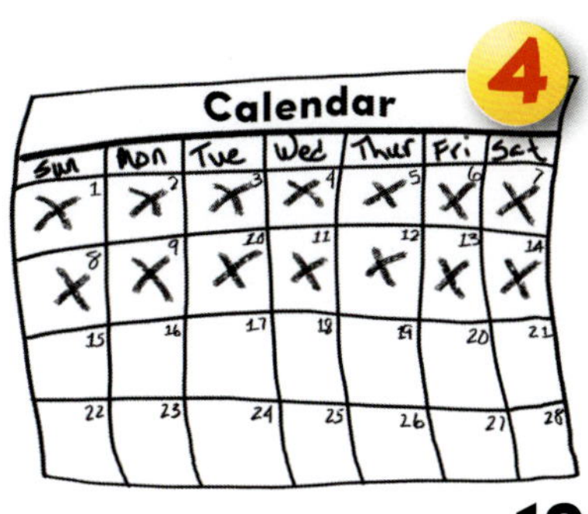

Glossary

plants—living things that use sunlight to grow

seeds—parts of plants that hold what is needed to start new plants

Index

Your Turn!

Get a seed and break it open. Draw what you see inside the seed. Try this with other seeds!

Consultants

Sally Creel, Ed.D.
Curriculum Consultant

Leann Iacuone, M.A.T., NBCT, ATC
Riverside Unified School District

Jill Tobin
California Teacher of the Year
Semi-Finalist
Burbank Unified School District

Publishing Credits

Conni Medina, M.A.Ed., *Managing Editor*
Lee Aucoin, *Creative Director*
Diana Kenney, M.A.Ed., NBCT, *Senior Editor*
Lynette Tanner, *Editor*
Lexa Hoang, *Designer*
Hillary Dunlap, *Photo Editor*
Rachelle Cracchiolo, M.S.Ed., *Publisher*

Image Credits: p.3 Geoffrey Kidd/Alamy; pp.5, 16–17 iStock; pp.18–19 (illustrations) Rusty Kinnunen; all other images from Shutterstock.

Library of Congress Cataloging-in-Publication Data

Austen, Elizabeth (Elizabeth Charlotte), author.
Seeds / Elizabeth Austen.
pages cm
Summary: "It is time to learn how seeds grow."—Provided by publisher.
Audience: K to grade 3.
Includes index.
ISBN 978-1-4807-4522-3 (pbk.) —
ISBN 978-1-4807-5131-6 (ebook)
1. Seeds—Juvenile literature. 2. Readers (Primary) I. Title.
QK661.A97 2015
575.6'8—dc23
2014008613

Teacher Created Materials
5301 Oceanus Drive
Huntington Beach, CA 92649-1030
http://www.tcmpub.com

ISBN 978-1-4807-4522-3

Printed in China 51497